$15.95 05

Everyday Character Education

Tolerance

by Connie Colwell Miller

Consultant:
Madonna Murphy, PhD, Professor of Education
University of St. Francis, Joliet, Illinois
Author, *Character Education in America's Blue Ribbon Schools*

Capstone
press
Mankato, Minnesota

First Facts is published by Capstone Press,
151 Good Counsel Drive, P.O. Box 669, Mankato, Minnesota 56002.
www.capstonepress.com

Library of Congress Cataloging-in-Publication Data
Miller, Connie Colwell, 1976–
    Tolerance / Connie Colwell Miller.
    p. cm.—(First facts. Everyday character education)
    Summary: "Introduces tolerance through examples of everyday situations where this
character trait can be used"—Provided by publisher.
    Includes bibliographical references and index.
    ISBN 0-7368-4282-9 (hardcover)
    1. Toleration—Juvenile literature. I. Title. II. Series.
BJ1431.M55 2006
179'.9—dc22   2004026313

Editorial Credits
Becky Viaene, editor; Molly Nei, set designer; Kate Opseth, book designer;
    Kelly Garvin, photo researcher/photo editor

Photo Credits
Capstone Press/Karon Dubke, cover, 1, 4, 5, 6–7, 8–9, 10, 11, 19, 21
Corbis/Ariel Skelley, 12–13; Jose Luis Pelaez Inc., 20
Gay Block, 1998, from Rescuers, Portraits of Moral Courage in the Holocaust, by Gay Block and
    Malka Drucker, Holmes & Me, 17
Photo courtesy of Ronda and Nickole Evans, 15

1 2 3 4 5 6 10 09 08 07 06 05

Table of Contents

Tolerance

Tony invites Sue to his house for lunch. Tony offers Sue a hot dog. Sue explains that she doesn't eat meat.

4

Tony is tolerant. He **accepts** that
people are different. Tony and Sue
eat macaroni and cheese instead
of hot dogs.

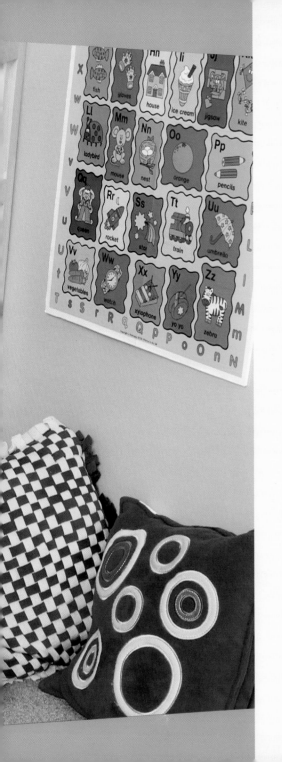

At Your School

School is a good place to show tolerance. Once a week, Tony's class listens to and helps younger children read.

Today, Tony is helping Jeff. Jeff reads more slowly than Tony. Tony knows that everyone reads at different speeds. Tony is **patient** while Jeff reads.

Fact!

At school, be tolerant of other students who learn more slowly or quickly than you do.

With Your Friends

Show your friends tolerance by accepting them. Your friend Josh is in a wheelchair and likes to play catch. You and your friends were going to jump rope. You decide to play catch instead, so Josh can play too.

Fact!
People with physical disabilities can play many sports. They can ski, swim, ride bicycles, and more.

At Home

You show you care about your
family when you are tolerant. You
and your brother like different music.
But you are willing to listen to his CD.

You and your family are watching a
football game. Not everyone cheers for
the same team as you. You are tolerant
when someone cheers for another team.

12

In Your Community

Tolerance makes your **community** a good place for everyone to live. People of different **races** and **religions** may live in your community. You can show all people **respect**. Tolerance of the differences of others helps everyone get along.

Fact!
International Day of Tolerance is celebrated on November 16.

Nickole Evans

Tolerant people help others. In just one year, Nickole Evans **volunteered** 500 hours. She taught people with disabilities how to use the Internet. Nickole also helped create an Internet site. The site taught kids to be friends with people of different races.

Fact!
In 1999, Nickole earned the Global Youth Peace and Tolerance Award.

Marie Taquet

Sometimes it takes great courage to be tolerant. Marie Taquet lived during World War II (1939–1945). At that time, German soldiers were killing many Jewish people.

Taquet was not Jewish, but she was tolerant of other faiths. She helped 80 Jewish boys hide from soldiers.

Fact!
In 1988, the boys who Marie Taquet hid met to honor and thank her for saving their lives.

What Would You Do?

Sam wears shoes that are different from Tony's and Phil's shoes. Phil laughs and points at Sam's shoes. How could Tony help Phil show tolerance?

Fact!

Many schools teach students a program called "Don't Laugh at Me." It teaches people not to tease or put down others.

Amazing but True!

About one-fifth of all U.S. people speak a language other than English at home. With tolerance, people are patient with others who speak a different language. They can live together happily.

Hands On: Learning Tolerance

You can learn about tolerance by thinking about other people's opinions and beliefs.

What You Need

three friends
    or family members
four pieces of paper
four markers

What You Do

1. Ask each person to answer the following questions on a sheet of paper. You answer the questions too. What is your favorite food? What is your favorite hobby? What is your favorite type of music?
2. Collect the sheets of paper.
3. Read each list.
4. Think about the answers. How do these things make everyone different? How do they make people the same?
5. Assign a weekday to each person in the group. On each person's day, eat their favorite food, participate in their favorite hobby, and listen to their favorite type of music.
6. When everyone has had a special day, think about what you learned by trying different things.

Glossary

accept (ak-SEPT)—to agree that someone is okay the way they are

community (kuh-MYOO-nuh-tee)—a group of people who live in the same area

patient (PAY-shuhnt)—waiting calmly without getting angry or upset

race (RAYSS)—a major group into which humans can be divided; people of the same race share a physical appearance, such as skin color.

religion (ri-LIJ-uhn)—a set of spiritual beliefs that people follow

respect (ri-SPEKT)—to believe in the quality and worth of others and yourself

volunteer (vol-uhn-TEEHR)—to offer to do a job, usually without pay

Read More

Raatma, Lucia. *Tolerance*. Character Education. Mankato, Minn.: Bridgestone Books, 2000.

Scheunemann, Pam. *Tolerance*. United We Stand. Edina, Minn.: ABDO, 2003.

Internet Sites

FactHound offers a safe, fun way to find Internet sites related to this book. All of the sites on FactHound have been researched by our staff.

Here's how:
1. Visit *www.facthound.com*
2. Type in this special code **0736842829** for age-appropriate sites. Or enter a search word related to this book for a more general search.
3. Click on the **Fetch It** button.

FactHound will fetch the best sites for you!

Index